Freedom of Movement
Reuben Lane

To Martyn,

It's been a few years we've known each other. Thank you for all your love and wisdom over all that time.

For Christina Dunhill

Some mysteries waiting to be discovered

Loads of Love

Reuben Lane

First published 2019

Copyright © Reuben Lane, 2019

Printed in London by Calverts

Editor: Christina Petrie

ISBN: 978-1-9162167-0-9

Lyttelton Stalls foyer, National Theatre. 22/9/18.

A voice rendered metallic over a security guard's walkie talkie. The House Manager strides across the foyer carpet after the second interval muttering to himself "ripped trousers; ripped seat; ripped everything." The bell rings behind the Long Bar. Brrr: pause; Brrr: pause; Brrr... The elderly old school barman carries a mandolin wrapped in a quilted nylon cover on his arched back. The cleaner pushes the vacuum cleaner across the carpet, picking up the percussion of dropped nuts and the cymbal splash of trodden-on crisps. Saturday night – Tony and Pat doing their big Egyptian number upstairs on the Olivier stage – a live milk snake with stage fright. "Not an iota of chemistry between them," muttered a father to his teenage son as they came out from the Gents at the end of their one interval. Saturday night – the hum of the vacuum cleaner wends towards me – the young Polish cleaner who two years ago blew up at me for putting the folded-up ice cream boxes in the bin and ever since has played a game of will he won't he acknowledge me whenever our paths cross – his polythene bags of ice-cream cartons, discarded newspapers and general unnecessary wrapping paraphernalia ballooned in his hands or dragged along the carpet. Saturday night at the Movies. Whigfield. Bananarama. Katrina and the Waves. The tops of glass tumblers shimmering like the silvery foam on a babbling mountain brook. My fellow usher – a formidably French woman with a broken foot strapped in bandage – her crutches resting against the leaflet rack – reading a book – the front cover folded under the back as she runs the fingers of her other hand through her long black hair.

Dementia beckons: Come here. Come over here and play with me. Don't be afraid – I'm a lot more fun than you might think.

And then unlock my bike – out of here by a quarter to eleven – along the Quiet Way Route One, home to Joseph's in Deptford – or rather back to my home in Joseph. Bermondsey. Snap-on Tools. Screwfix; the warehouses with their crenellated sides – the blind person bumps on the edges of the pavement. Bleep. The clatter of ice cubes into a metal champagne bucket. Hoovers. Let's Dance – under the moonlight, the serious moonlight. Chess moves – two squares forward and one to the side of the knight. The cunning rook with his flask of Rohypnol-laced brandy. "Just a sip." A slip. "Check." "Huh?" "Checkmate." The same show on repeat.

The mice run for it across the carpet – scuttle into the ventilation grate. On the site of an ancient plague pit.

The veteran (but new to here – a summer recruit) splurges the slab of the bar with purple antiseptic spray, swirling circles with a paper towel. And then our love will climb the bowers and pop its flowers, just before the cull of autumn, in the nick of time – limbs melding. The empty bottle trolley across the brick hard floor. A trumpet tootling mellow jazz muzack in preparation for the post-show diners in the restaurant. Cleopatra's asp. Her scented barge.

Last glasses collected. A head tipped – mobile flat against his ear. The House Manager at the box office surfing the net. The sea surge of applause breaks on this island. This island breaks.

Finsbury Park. 28/9/18.

And so today I do get to Finsbury Park to sit beneath the lime and
lemon coloured leaves of the planes. A brown ball of seeds the size
of a lychee waiting on this bench for me to pocket and take with me
to put on the bookshelf of my temporary new room in Earlsfield.

This morning, taking shirts and trousers off the hangers in the IKEA
wardrobe in my bedroom. Folding them over and piling them up
inside a giant raffia plastic carry-all. Stuffing the sides with t-shirts,
underpants and socks, deferring the promised cull of ragged and
holey items. Boxing up my printer. And going through the nine-
inch scurf of leaflets; bank statements; hospital letters; sex club
polythene bags each containing a single foil-wrapped condom and
sachet of lubricant; old and new batteries; bicycle lamps; brake
pads and coins all piled up on my tabletop. Amongst all this, the ICA
cinema stub from *Loveless* on February 14th – my first date with
Joseph – the memory of how I spotted him as I came into the foyer
through the sliding glass doors from the Mall. There he was, ten
minutes early, bent browsing over a table of books – and I slipped
into the Gents for a pee before he could look up to see me. That
electric moment when halfway through the movie he slunk down
in the seat next to me and rested his head against my shoulder. And
still, these seven and a half months later, the same excitement – still
the wonder of us being together and the bond gradually growing
even stronger.

A parade of folk outlined in sunshine passing along the tarmac
road down the hill. A Spanish skateboarder, a black sleeper in
his earlobe, bends his shorts-exposed knees to loop down the
lumpy slope. A mother in spangled lycra pushes a buggy hooped
with Bags For Life shopping. The sites that I'll miss: the Turkish
and Kurdish shops and restaurants on Grand Parade; the solace
of Railway Fields; the ginnel of Harringay Passage; this park, my
favourite in the whole world so far.

Finsbury Park. 1/10/18.

"Goodbye house," I call out in the living room as I'm about to leave. A final check – my cotton tote bag that I have stuffed with some dirty underwear; a couple of carrots, a root of ginger; a towel; a paperback (*Mr Clive And Mr Page* by Neil Bartlett) that I rescued from Ari's because I want to read it a second time – the first time – I check the publication date – my goodness – 1996 – and I lent it to Mum who really enjoyed it – its evocation of working in a 1950s London department store that felt accurate with her memories of working as a window-dresser at Bourne and Hollingsworth in the late 40s and early 50s; a hand mirror (or did I forget that? I think I might have done – left it on the bathroom sink); my knapsack laden with my sleeping bag and sundry odds and ends (two tablets of washing powder; a pebble with a hole through it from Folkestone beach if I remember correctly – Boris and I's last visit to the Triennial; toothbrush and razor). And then I decide to unbolt the back door and step down into the rubble-strewn yard – the walled lip up onto the grass (a sunflower head hit me on the side of the face this morning as I cycled from Joseph's – on the road opposite the end of Deptford High Street – the sunflower poking out behind a buddleia – an almighty Whack that made me wonder at the incredible mathematics of Nature – how a heavyweight flowerhead like that can come from a single sunflower seed). The peace on that hillside, all those empty gardens, boxes of sunshine. And then I went back inside, slotted up the bolt, and stepped onto the front doorstep – the melamine front door sealing shut behind me – my two single Yale keys left inside. Step down the five steps, unlock my bike cabled to the front gate, wrap the cotton handle of my tote bag around the handlebars so that it won't rub and snag against the top of the front wheels, and, pushing off, freewheel down the hill of Beresford Road one final euphoric time. A grubby dusty house. The potential of my now ex-bedroom revealed once more when emptied of all my clobber – the sunshine pouring in from the garden – the branches of the sycamore bordering with the garden behind.

The boxes I lifted with Ari's help up into the rafters of Karsten's attic this morning, me heaving them up the stepladder and Ari leaning down and pulling them up from above. "The real tragedy is," said

Ari as we'd nearly finished, "all of this will eventually end up in the skip." Karsten, a little kinder, tells me to put boxes of anything papery (photos, letters, Edith's manuscripts) under his bed in case they get damp in the attic.

Leicester Square. 12/10/18.

Five young men with a boombox and a microphone out busking in the north-east corner of Leicester Square. A rope on the ground boxes off a stage.

"Come closer. We're going to do a show for you in a couple of minutes' time. Don't be afraid. We're just black. And actually two of these guys are only half black – which makes one white – which is something you can relate to. Ha ha. Come on – make some noise. Because the most important thing is your energy. No energy..."

"NO SHOW!" the other four shout back.

"Come on. Let me all hear y'all shout yeah!"

"Yeah," comes from a few American tourists lacklustredly.

"That was crap. Come on – shout YEAH!"

"Yeah!" This time a little louder.

"Right! Now shout yeah, I'm going to give you all my money."

Silence.

"HA HA HA."

Leicester Square. That hollow hub of the West End that always feels as if it should be gaudier, more light-spangled, more glamorous, edgier. THE ONLY DARKNESS IS IGNORANCE, on the marble scroll of the statue of William Shakespeare – one elbow leaning on a pile of books – the crown of his head and the mantle of his cloak balanced with three pigeons scrubbing at themselves.

The frontage of the Odeon Leicester Square ripped off. The original bricks from the 1930s revealed behind the cladding. A hole open to the elements where the foyer entrance and first floor bar used to be. The slope of the Circle held up by a framework of iron beams – lassoed coils of red cable hanging beneath the ceiling.

Two teenage boys doing stunts on their skateboards. A young woman walking purposefully – in each hand a clear carrier bag holding three big boxes each of a dozen Dunkin' Donuts – 72 doughnuts in total. Death by Donuts. ·

Start this. See this. Sear this. Suture this. Sure this. Sleek speckled starlings nip in and beat the bigger more cumbersome pigeons to the strips of sandwich bread thrown behind them by a group of French teenage boys sitting on the benches.

A voice offers urgent instructions in Polish over the crackle of a workman's walkie talkie – sitting in dust-imbued trousers and work boots on the other side of this plane tree – the tinny instructions mingling with the workman's cigarette smoke getting wafted straight up my nostrils.

Clapham Common. 24/10/18.

This version of the soul plays its part after dark on the Common. The line of epiphany trees that cloak the footpath from the bandstand to the top of the long hill that leads down to Battersea. Those semi-mythical rides from the swimming pool in Brixton to Battersea Park; reading Virginia Woolf in the lamplight along the riverfront, circa 1992-93. Earlier visits – to Le Grand Café, down the far end of the Common towards Clapham Junction, an occasional birthday treat with Mum, Dad and my sister; to my friend Roseanna's, whose housemate once got beaten up here on the Common at night. To now (will become a part of the movie in my head) cycling back to Earlsfield in the dark.

The homeless man with dreadlocks who keeps his belongings under the open roof of the council outbuilding by the pond; the squadron of Canada geese all pitched on the grass rooting through the soil; 'Madeleine', the patisserie where the black Frenchman elegantly makes me a coffee with a bagged-up almond croissant that I then sit to eat and drink beside the Alpha Course church (no fear that I might anytime soon get sucked inside to sign up to speak in tongues and overidentify with Jesus Christ, my Lord and Saviour). The shellac-black crows pulling out litter from the bins. Or, even more suitably, the single magpie who lands silently a couple of feet from my shoes – the velvet of the black feathers on its head and neck giving way to a streak of metallic blue and a wedge, when the sun glances against it, of emerald green – and stops to beady-eye me:

"You can talk! You're the worst thief of all. A writer who says he's writing about his own life – but steals his friends' stories without their permission. Until they cotton on and ditch you. Ha ha ha ha," the magpie clacks, "perhaps you should have a bell on a collar around your neck. BEWARE. WRITER COMING!"

The all-night SNACK WAGON that smells unappetizingly of fried onions and cheap sausages. The tent of the Moscow State Circus that has pitched there for this week. From here a bus to Crystal Palace – perhaps I'll go and visit the Crystal Palace Master; ring his doorbell; he'll usher me in: "How are you boy?" and once I've caught my breath and drunk a glass of water he'll lead me through to his bedroom and order: "Strip, boy," and snap his fingers for me to kneel in front of where he's sat on the edge of the bed. I'll tip my head forward and he'll clasp the leather collar around my neck. "Have you been missing me, boy?" The crazy, slightly ridiculous, but still erotic thrill of being a 52 year old man into an occasional intense session of roleplay BDSM. Crystal Palace – the sports stadium where my sister and I went swimming. The dinosaurs in the park. The Billy Graham rally in the stadium Mum and I went to one Sunday summer evening – a self-aggrandising millionaire showman – nothing more – spirituality for shopping mall devotees. Back in South London where I grew up – all to discover through careful reappraisal how I became the man I am – and why I didn't become the man I'm not.

Clapham Common, by the temporary metal wall of
Winterville. 2/11/18.

I try to get to where I sat a fortnight ago – the flock of a hundred
Canada geese chewing on the grass – but today that patch of the
Common is surrounded by another of the iron-plated riveted
walls that I fumed against just yesterday in Hyde Park – this one
for a similar commercial venture – Winterville. So I park my back
up against a green panel that bends backwards with a satisfying
metallic rumble.

Joseph wrote in his brief email last night of travelling on the train
from Lisbon to Évora across 'a strange and foreign land' – his
parents waiting for him brilliantly and delightfully at the station.
Those warm hugs must have been something to behold.

And how south-west London is a strange and foreign land to
me. Two afternoons ago I cycled up the long street of posh villas
between Wandsworth and Clapham Commons – and hundreds of
rich white children decked in ghoulish costumes and whitepan
facepaint paraded from door to door – trick or treating – cotton
cobwebs across hedges and candlelit carved pumpkins on walls
– accompanied by just as many adults who would watch from
the pavements parked full of Range Rovers. The open front doors
were swamped with children several lines deep delving into the
proffered bucket of sweets. "It's all gone mad around here!" a black
woman yelled into her mobile, her look of disgust the only one that
made sense to me. What if a door was opened by a frail old man or
woman who had dementia? What would those guardian adults do if
someone asked for their help?

And then this morning I returned to Tooting Broadway after
abandoning my search for Aldi yesterday to the tumbling rain. Back
along the grungey Garratt Lane – and this time I got it!

Tooting Broadway. A bronze statue of Edward VII outside the tube
station. The ancient pale green and cream Victorian lampposts.
Fingerposts – one way to Wimbledon, the other to London. And not
just the gleaming Germanic aisles of Aldi, but, on either side, the

Tooting Arcade and the Broadway Arcade. Chinese herbalist and acupuncturist – Indian fabrics – Caribbean saltfish and tilapia in a metal dish steaming with spices and chunks of lime – a cocktail bar with a giant rainbow flag that I'll take Joseph and Seta to.

My last visit to 'a strange and foreign land' – for now – when cycling back from work along the Thames Path – the river shining like the shiniest Saturday night TV show's floor – and coming inland at Wandsworth Bridge, I stop (breaking my usual ethical code) for a midnight 'deluxe' vegetable burger and fries at the Drive Thru McDonalds – the order taken by a cute moon-faced blond Polish lad – the place packed almost entirely with men – cabbies and boozers – and workers like the Romanian plasterer arguing with his employer to be paid properly into his mobile: "I'm going to eat now. And then I'll see how I feel – I'm wrecked now. If I'm OK – then I'll come back."

Harleyford Road Community Garden, Vauxhall. 3/11/18.

Sometimes you get stuck on long winding stories that are not that interesting.

I sit Saturday morning in these gardens, buzzing from a coffee from the store opposite the Bonnington Café – the back streets jungled by squatters from the early 80s. A fig tree, a banana tree, holly and yew. Handfuls of leaves knocked down from the trees. In a back garden over the fence, the reassuring sound of a spade shovelling earth, scraping just beneath the surface.

The bedraggled leaves of a silver birch tree. A helicopter overhead landing on the roof of the MI5 building. A retaining flowerbed wall made of red clay tiles moulded into the shapes of a thistle, a Tudor rose and a three leaf clover.

Charlie, the owner of the store, playing a fiddle between serving customers. "Would you like to take one of our newsletters?" he asks when I pay for my coffee.

"Would you take some of my homemade pamphlets to sell?"

"What are they about?" he asked, applying some resin to his bow.

"Oh – I'm not quite sure yet. I haven't made them. Perhaps they'd simply be a trail across a day of the year. Some of it might be explicit; drug and sexual references – perhaps you'd have to sell them in a brown paper bag? I could photocopy a drawing on the cover and paint each one in."

I think of Boris in his garden – how I should bring him here – have lunch at the Bonnington Café – then surprise him with this garden tucked along a tunnel through a Georgian terrace. Those glorious times when he had the bungalow further down the road in Golders Green – and he would be gardening – and I would sit on the back steps writing as he wrestled up deep-rooted weeds, ferried wheelbarrows of dead foliage across the garden – my duty to stop, make a pot of tea and bring it out with a plate of Garibaldi biscuits.

Orange berries and fecund shrubbery; Angela Carter prose. A tabby cat with white-booted paws tiger-prowls along the top of the fence, mingling with the haws of the tied-back rose bush. Blooms of velvety moss in the interstices of the slats of this gently rotting bench.

Nothing stays the same. Nothing lasts forever.

Everything stays the same. Everything lasts forever. Leave your benevolent mark.

Boris's current garden made beside the scarring fury and dementia-inducing smog of the North Circular – a gift to the drivers and pedestrians – those who look out and up – of Golders Green.

Win back the space. Make our utopias happen. Fight with books in our hands.

Russell Square. 8/11/18.

Coming through the wall, just ten minutes after Joseph had turned his bedside lamp out, a searing hot row between the couple we have heard arguing before. The man (English) yelling at her with scorn and disgust – every sentence beginning with "You fucking…" Every time he yelled fucking he compressed it into the tightest wodge of pure undistilled hatred – as if spitting in her face. She (Italian or Spanish) screaming that she'd had enough – that this time she was leaving for good. He: "Well fucking get out. It's my fucking property." And she mocking him: "Yeah? Call the police. Call the police. Call the police."

And Joseph and I lay there holding onto one another. Both of us – I sensed – tensing to bound out of bed, skid across the hall rug, open the front door and bang at their next door, should the man's verbal fury cross the line into a physical attack.

After half an hour of repetitive volcanic explosions: "You fucking bitch." "Call the police!" – the wall became silent. I knocked my hand against the hardboard panel – and felt in the deep bass echo how empty the hollow interior was.

This morning Joseph woke me with kisses on the back of my neck, spooning up against me. "Your alarm call," he whispered.

"I didn't realise that that rowing couple lived just next door through the wall," I said.

"They don't," he said, "they live on the ground floor. That's what I mean – the insulation in these walls is terrible. And sound travels throughout the block."

"But we could hear virtually every word they said. It sounded as if it was coming from just the other side of this wall."

"But it wasn't."

"Did you hear them last night?" asked Flo, Joseph's flatmate at breakfast, "I'm really sorry about that."

"No," said Joseph, "it's not your fault at all. It's just unfortunate."

"It's because they have mice. That's what they were arguing about."

"Mice? Really?" I was sceptical – as Joseph and I climbed the two flights of stairs down to the front door of the block – "it didn't sound like they were shouting about having mice."

"No," said Joseph, "it sounded as if they were shouting because they really hated each other."

Red Lion Square, Holborn. 10/11/18.

Saturday morning. Early.

"Sorry. I'm not ready. The machine's still warming up." The cheerful barista at the coffee stall in Deptford Waste Market.

"Surely your mum and dad would love to experience this? All the stuff they can't buy in Melbourne."

Joseph screws up his face: "What – a skateboard? All this junk. An old VCR that's got rained on?"

"A complete set of hardback Stephen Kings?"

"Go that way!" – a stallholder lifts his heavy frame up into the driver's seat of his van, blocking our path. We climb over the trailer where it hitches onto the back of the van. A man steering a barrow of Huggies disposable nappies coming through. "Please put them back. We're not ready yet," he tells the West African man seizing up an armful of the packs.

Harleyford Road Community Garden, Vauxhall. 11/11/18.

In spite of the rain. In spite of the grief.

Donald Trump stays in his Parisian hotel room flicking through the porn channels on satellite TV – looking for a glimpse of the woman he loves most in the world, Stormy Daniels. "I can't come," he bellows, sitting on the edge of the emperor-size bed, his black trousers down around his ankles as Melania taps at the intervening door between their suites and coos through the keyhole: "But darling – we have to go. The motorcade is waiting to take us to the ceremony at Belleau. The boy Emmanuel and Mutti Merkel are already there waiting for us."

"But it's raining. Donald J Trump doesn't do rain. I'll send a tweet instead."

He pumps his pumpkin-hued penis. A wriggle of blood worms its way along its arteries as he catches a glimpse of a blonde woman in the back of the TV. "Ah dammit." His cock goes completely limp as the shaky digital camera pans in to reveal it is a woman who not even in a million years he could kid his brain was Stormy.

"Tell Manu I'll see him for a round of golf after he gets back from the boneyard. And tell him the loser sucks dick."

Melania puts her ear flush against the polished oak. "What was that?" She listens hard. "Ugh!" She gets up from her knees – something damp on the carpet. A stream of very yellow urine seeps through the doorway. "DT? Cuddles? Are you OK?"

The President's voice articulates a series of loud gasps as if he is being pummeled in the stomach.

"Darling! I'm coming in. Baron!" Melania clicks her fingers for her son to put down his 'Ken does Crystal Meth Lab' doll and go and get the security detail stationed in the lobby.

The door is busted down. And there lies the President of the United States flat on his face – his trousers around his ankles – in a pile of piss and diarrhoea. Stormy Daniels' face in close up freeze-framed on the huge TV, her eyes boring into the room, her top lip curled up in disdain.

Harleyford Road Gardens, Vauxhall. 15/11/18.

Exactly halfway through my three-month stay in Earlsfield. And I wonder if this isn't the way to go about the precarious expensive business of renting and sharing in London? To just embrace the uncertainty and keep moving on to temporary lets – two or three months, even a few weeks at a time.

What amazes me is how quickly the new begins to feel familiar. For instance my cycle route up beside Wandsworth Cemetery, turning beside the Victorian prison, across the Common, stopping at 'Madeleine' for a croissant, putting it in my bag, cycling on – and just along from the floodlights of the Oval cricket ground locking up my bike on the railings at Bonnington Gardens – getting a coffee from Charlie, who already knows me by sight – taking coffee and croissant in here, the secret Harleyford Road Gardens clothed in fallen leaves. And I think maybe we've got it completely wrong – this human ideal of making ourselves a home where we surround ourselves with familiar objects and smells – a burrow, safe from the outside world – and instead we should keep moving; eternal migrants caravanning, sailing and walking from place to place; sampling the unfamiliar; adapting to different habitats.

Yesterday Theresa May published her Brexit plan: a sheaf of 350 printed pages in which she sacrifices everything else in order to curtail freedom of movement for EU citizens in the UK – and that of UK citizens in the EU.

I have the sense that by staying in a place for a short time I become more adventurous; go out and explore more; make connections; the roots grow down deep in a very short amount of time. While, when I stay in the same house and area, my brain tunnels inwards – I grow insular and fearful of losing what I have. And strangely I am most fearful of losing the places I am least happy in.

So I will move along. I will indeed go with Joseph to stay with his family for Passover in Melbourne in five months' time.

I won't be afraid of how and where and with whom I'll be moving in the New Year.

Butterfield Green, Dalston. 18/11/18.

The doggy folk of Dalston gather with their canine rulers on the dewy grass of Butterfield Green. Sunday morning. The trees winnow their leaves; the next few days going from glorious finery to tattered rags. That long summer heatwave furnishing them in the widest range of deep true colours that can't help but open up a space inside your chest for wonder.

Virginia Woolf minus that final despair. The two lads dribbling a slightly flat baseball on the court in the corner. The tarmac under a coat of leaves gone slimy taking away the clean ringing echo of summer or ice cold winter.

"Are you going away for Christmas?" the two last dog-owners, a man and a woman, both of whom are London Turkish, as they separate towards opposite gates off the Green.

"We don't really do Christmas," she calls back.

"No – but it's still a holiday."

"And we do put up a Christmas tree."

Leg of Mutton Woodland, Thames Path, Putney. 23/11/18.

A grey damp fug. Getting off the 44 bus on Putney Bridge
and walking along the south side – a row of boathouses each
emblazoned with the loud regalia and names of various public
schools: Westminster, Dulwich College, Emmanuel.

And when the road becomes a proper path going through trees with
a thick glorious stink of leaf mulch, I realise that a lot of my troubled
thoughts over the past few days have been the self-eating thoughts
of self-hatred – of doubt in my ability to be a good partner to Joseph
– the phantom of erotic sex with the guy on the fourteenth floor in
Southfields coming in to nix my chance of a life-lasting love and true
compatibility – and that I simply needed to do this – to get out and
walk for the day – long strides; the hit of raw ozone clearing the
pipes of my brain.

The book of connections. Walking this stretch of the Thames
with Maude – picnics in Kew Gardens – the sandstone Harrods
Furniture Depository, converted into expensive apartments since
I was last here – the Riverside Studios (once the artistic home to
the playwright and director, Peter Gill, who sent me a short letter
encouraging my writing when I was 23) – the green iron Victorian
chinoiserie of Hammersmith Bridge spooling across this wide
stretch of river. Hammersmith where once, the summer of 1985,
having dropped a tab of Albert's acid, I floated high, my vision
colour-drenched and doodle-enhanced, early Sunday morning
around Shepherd's Bush.

Rowing teams sculling on the river. A middle-aged man in wellington
boots hauls himself over the side of a motor launch where he has
fallen down the fifteen foot bank trying to retrieve his terrier. "We're
effecting a rescue," the woman at the prow of the motor launch
says – four oarsmen breaking stroke and putting their paddles out
perpendicular to stop. "Are you alright?" the harbour master calls
from his tug. "There's some steps back along there." The woman at the
prow points upstream. The man's wife up on the path – the lead to the
terrier looped around a branch – "Okey dokey, we'll see you there."

And I realise it's fine – great – splendid – to crunch together all the complexities of being an older gay man in the year 2018; the possibilities of love and sex – or love or sex, or sex simply on its own – and with Joseph, who, younger and more intelligent, is able to crack open my worries and help me find the solutions inside the problems. The honesty of our desires – perverse, greedy, counterintuitive; society's homophobic fear-inducing taboos brought out into the open; 'queer' tagged and celebrated; shame and guilt only hexing happiness and fulfilment.

Wandsworth Cemetery. 25/11/18.

Sitting on a small two-seater wooden bench lichened and
splattered with bird shit on the bank beside the railway siding
silenced for Sunday engineering works. A squabble of seagulls
down over the tops of the gravestones. Two marble tablets in the
shapes of teddy bears.

This seat commemorates three of the Ledgley family. Sarah Jane,
1864–1945; Frank, 1858–1927 and Leonard Charles, 1893–1946,
'BURIED IN PAUPERS GRAVE UNDER HERE.' This now the turning
circle for motorist mourners to drive thru, having dropped off
their wreaths and crinkle plastic wrapped bouquets. Some HAPPY
BIRTHDAY banners splayed along the railings, a silver helium
balloon on a piece of string. Consciences salved. A Jamaican man's
gravestone etched with the dates of his SUNRISE and SUNSET into
the pristine polished marble. The motorist mourners drive back out
through the cemetery gates.

I should make a will. Write down how I don't want to end up buried
in a cemetery – but rather in a cardboard box under a forest or
a field of soon-to-be-planted tree saplings. Punch the clock – the
winnings from the conveyor belt – 'Didn't he do well?' Not for me –
as close to empty when I die as possible. I'll leave my inheritance in
these notebooks. The roots supping on my bones.

Back now to prepare Sunday lunch with Emily at the house here
in Earlsfield. A fruit salad. Peel and dice the potatoes and carrots.
Joseph coming over by bus. A sullen sky. A steady stream of traffic –
headlamps on – filtering in from the side road – the hill up towards
Wandsworth Common. Oscar Wilde's prison. Looking to move on.
Where happens next? Spraying a spritz of GHB into their/his/her
orange juice; overdosing into a coma; cardiac arrest; death. And
thus I die and cry and cry and die – and split and break up – the
dividends of a melting world. The hope resists being believed in.
Love traded in for something bleaker and more comfortable. Winter
Sunday in the cemetery. The damp cold blanketing the sounds. A
parakeet's shrieks gnawing scars into my brain.

British Film Institute foyer mezzanine gallery. 26/11/18.

OK – let's do this – some family therapy. Pull up your chairs into a circle, gather around.

Like a greenhouse glowing with lights – but instead of orchids, a grapevine or marijuana plants this glass room propagated books.

The door into the small crowded bookshop in Nunhead opened inwards – and a couple of women had to stand and shuffle their chairs out of the way to allow Joseph and me to sidle into the shop. The owner of the shop waved us in from behind the counter: "Welcome. Welcome. Grab a seat." "Do you want our names?" I waved a finger at the printed list as I shrugged off my black leather jacket. "No no no. We're about to make a start." Someone got up to offer me a seat in the front – the tips of my shoes just a few inches away from Julián Fuks' impressive shiny blue trousers and just beneath his long shaggy brown beard. Joseph filled a gap in the row in the window next to a woman in a bumblebee yellow winter coat.

Boyd Tonkin asked Julián Fuks about his novel *Resistance* – whether he considered it autofictive (yes, he did); about the ethics of writing about his family; and in particular about his adopted brother ("Ethics are indeed precisely what are involved"). About the forms of resistance his parents were involved in during the Dirty War in Argentina – and that he and the Brazilians who aren't one of the 55 million who recently voted in Jair Bolsonaro as President can take part in now. ("In truth, I and the cultured left are not those most at risk. The most vulnerable are the most vulnerable – the poorest people in the favelas; the young black men who are targeted and killed by the police in huge numbers – and who will be targeted even more now that they feel they have been mandated to do so by a leader who names torturers amongst his personal heroes"). About the many people who approach Las Abuelas de Plaza de Mayo who were born during the years of the military dictatorship in Argentina and want a blood DNA test to see if they might actually be one of the 500 children born in captivity and subsequently adopted. "'Why do you think you might be adopted?' they ask them. 'Because I have nothing in common with my parents' they often reply. Which is when the Abuelas say 'But maybe you need to see a family therapist rather than do a DNA test?'"

Only once during the hour long discussion did I turn the 180 degrees to look behind me to smile at Joseph. His look back was rigid and anxious – I could tell he was worried about getting to the film at the Prince Charles Cinema before it started.

On Saturday morning Joseph had woken – his brain preoccupied with the email he had had the previous afternoon asking him to attend a compulsory meeting with the CEO at his other job. "Why?" he wailed, "they're obviously going to give me the sack." I tried to reassure him that this was very unlikely – a duty manager on a zero hours contract being called in to be personally sacked by the CEO. I poured Joseph a bowl of muesli and soya milk and added a handful of blueberries. Whilst I waited for my bagel to pop up from the toaster, Joseph squeezed some honey onto his cereal. As I pasted some Vegemite on the bagel Joseph took a spoonful of his muesli. "Ugh – UGH!" he hyperventilated and dashed over to the sink, taking a swig straight from the tap before spitting it back out. 'That's all a bit melodramatic,' I thought, 'for a mouldy blueberry.' "Are you OK?" "No no – I'm not," he spat some more, took another swig, washed his mouth out again and spat again, "I told you I was preoccupied. I thought I was putting honey on my muesli – but it wasn't – it was the washing up liquid. Didn't you see me do it?" "Yes – I saw you – I thought – squeezing the honey." "But it wasn't." "No – I realise. I'm sorry sweetheart. But at least it was Ecover and not Fairy Liquid." "Don't tell anyone about this."

I hugged Joseph. He is so adorable. Gently teasing him when he went to the toilet by whistling 'I'm Forever Blowing Bubbles'.

"I love you," I told him.

"I love you more."

"Hmmm? What does that mean?"

"Oh, it's just something Mum and I say."

Joseph led the way out of the bookshop. The door slammed behind me – the glass pane giving a brittle sneeze – I put my hand back behind me too late to break its fall. "You can't retrieve the sound of the banging door" – Joseph was hotfooting ahead of me, looking at the app on his phone –"come on – there's a bus coming in three minutes."

Belgrade Road café, Dalston. 27/11/18.

"You don't mind a Scottish fiver? It's still legal tender, although some people are funny about it. Well – thank you. Goodbye. Have a good day."

I look up, ready with a 'Take care' on my lips should he look my way as he steps towards the door – not wishing him to put me in the standoffish up-his-own-arse category. Gay and melancholy, in our fifties, me and him both – he probably used to come to the cinema in the nineties when I worked there. Nobody had a secret crush on me then – the cinema usher – or only one so secretive that it never, in the eleven years I worked there, revealed itself to me. The cinema that I passed on my way here; a new marquee light sign and some much needed new quad boxes for the movie posters – this week an enticing mix of Steve McQueen's *Widows*, Hirokazu Kore-eda's *Shoplifters* and Luca Guadagnino's *Suspiria*.

Yesterday afternoon I made my first ever visit to the Clapham Picturehouse for a matinee of *Shoplifters*. On entering Screen 4 an overwhelming, unmistakable smell of pee-sodden underclothes and sweet cloying perfume that I'll forever associate with the once-a-month OAP Classic Matinees we used to have at the cinema here in Dalston when the Hackney old people's homes were bussed in. That same redolent odour filled the auditorium and lingered long after we had opened both sets of fire doors at the end of the show to try and blow some fresh air through.

Shoplifters is about an ad hoc family of thieves and abducted orphans who are given house space by an elderly widowed woman who is scared of living out her last years on her own – a tight squeeze in a single room apartment in a shanty town on the edge of a Japanese city. Some intense quiet scenes near the end of the film when two of the thieves are being interrogated in a police cell were ruined when the soundtrack of the Queen movie *Bohemian Rhapsody* in the auditorium next door bellowed 'We are the champions' over the top of the Japanese dialogue.

Checking for the time – guessing at it – looking out for the school kids that will mean it's 3.30. Watching the features of a tall man walking past in an oat-coloured beanie hat – in his sixties by the stretched skin on his face – his right hand held out at his waist – a series of definite gestures – each of which he holds for several seconds before flipping onto the next one – talking to himself – a pep talk or a discussion on where to next in his life. I see the young man in his face and his upright posture but the old man in the way he is talking unabashed out aloud to himself through the rain – little imagining or indeed caring that he is being watched.

The music clicks off. Pipe, the Croatian proprietor, presses the button for a new track. Guitar and drums playing jazz. The silver birches in front of the church hall amongst the last to lose their yellow leaves. The soft beat of brushes against the drum's skin. Pipe's kind gesture – not hurrying me out after all the other customers have paid up and gone; giving the Long Read about anti-Semitism in France in today's Guardian Journal to the elderly man who asks if he can take it with him so that his wife can read it. "I want to read that too," Pipe says, "but I'll read it on my iPhone." "Are you sure?" asked the old man. "Of course – take it."

The light sucked up into the sky. Lights glowing in the arched windows of the Victorian Saint Matthias church.

St Matthew's Church Gardens, Brixton. 29/11/18.

Days will tip over – the same light – ampersands – amber
streetlamps – as that outside my grandparents' house in Chesham
that used to fall through the window of the bedroom halfway up the
staircase. Brixton – the gardens of St Matthew's Church – the tower
of Lambeth Town Hall – still home in my head to red Ted Knight
and Linda Bellos as leaders of the Council. And there behind me the
night club, called the Electric, that I know as The Fridge – that used
to have actual fridges up along the canopy – home to Acid House in
the 80s and Love Muscle in the 90s – and that before that used to be
a cinema: Jamaican movies – *Countryman* and *The Harder They Come*
lettered along the fractured lines of the Readograph sign when Dad
drove me to choir on Sunday mornings. And down the road there
used to be Morley's department store; opposite it, a Woolworths
where Mum once got so annoyed that the young woman at the till
served the customer on the other side – when she had been waiting
far longer – that she slammed the money down on the counter and,
with a "Come on!" to my sister and me, stormed off towards the steel
and glass doors. "That better be the right money," the sales assistant
called after her. The Bon Marché on the other side of the railway
bridge. Up a flight of stairs there had been an earlier incarnation of
The Fridge – a room of sweat-filled bodies dancing – not that I ever
saw that tighter, headier club myself – I only knew about it from
a short film I saw about it that must have shown at the Ritzy – oh,
those days – how important that cinema was to my late teens and
early twenties – a place Mum and I went to every week. Double bills
– quirky documentary guerrilla shorts – a whole full programme –
buying coffee and a slab of carrot or chocolate cake in the interval
– the left hand side of the auditorium Smoking; the right hand side,
Non. Multimillionairess Picturehouse Programme Director Clare
Binns sitting behind the Automaticket machine in the ticket booth.
And this spot – where I would get on the Number 2 or 2B bus to
Tulse Hill and West Norwood. Home unpeels from the memory.
What worthwhile sticks? Hyacinth Brown; I should really find out if
she's still around – living in Cormorant Court on Rosendale Road –
and take her a rum-soaked fruit cake and an armful of roses.

Old English Garden, Battersea Park. 30/11/18.

Hidden away – beyond the edge of the mount inside the picture
frame – behind an eight-foot brick wall and through a latch gate lies
this secret garden. Today – unsatisfied and disgruntled – a twist in
the guts that suggests too much coffee or some buried disquiet – I
abandon my quest to retrace the atmosphere of the river front,
of Battersea Park twenty five years ago – my hair still damp and
chlorine-smelling from the Brixton Rec pool – notebook and Virginia
Woolf novels on the go – the park back then – in the early 90s – a
more solitary place with occasional joggers and dogwalkers looming
out of the mist or rain at dusk beneath the wires of lightbulbs strung
between the Victorian lampposts along the embankment railings;
the Romance of then now dissipated by the sheer volume of entitled
posh folk chit-chatting loudly. The redbrick Chelsea mansion blocks
on the north side of the river that now only seem to be the domain
of corporate millionaires.

Red bricked paths around a pond. A fountain – a big stone bowl held
up by the tails of four goggle-eyed, fat-lipped stone fish; the falling
streams rattling against the surface of the pool. A cape of gingko
and maple leaves floating, waiting to sink and join the dark brown
sludgy murk two feet below. Wisteria and roses winding around the
wooden arboretum.

Pushing my bike along the riverfront, past the golden Buddha niched
in his huge Peace Pagoda, his forefinger and thumb held in that
A–OK circle – tangling with the inane self-absorbed conversation
of stupidly rich folk – and needing a pee – I remembered that my
chain needed a coat of oil, so I turned my bike upside down – resting
it on its handlebars – gave the chain a lick of oil and then noticed
how clogged up with mud, hairs and grit the chainset was; found
some twigs and poked and scraped the accretions loose – my hands
becoming smudged with black oil. I locked my bike to the railing,
went and washed my hands – ten minutes of soap dispenser pearly
pink gel and cold water only managing to make the stains a paler grey.
I took a pee; washed my hands again. And then thought – where is
that garden – that bit of this park I discovered when I was cycling to
visit Maude when she was slowly approaching her death in Kingston

Hospital – and that I found as if by invitation just that once and have never looked for since? I walked back, past the children's zoo and the Festival Gardens. The wall appeared like a lush memory lost and refound. I stepped inside. 'Yes – this was the place.'

Two young men swerve around on their bikes and sit for half an hour on the bench diagonally opposite – building themselves a relay of hashish-crumbled joints – the burning hash and tobacco wafting across the pool towards me. I try not to stare at them – neither wishing them to register my gaze as disapproval, or a yen to be offered a toke, or indeed an invitation to them to come across and ask me what I'm writing. After the half hour they climb on their bikes and let themselves out through the gate in the brick wall.

Schoolboys way off in the distance beyond the border of trees on the other side of the garden – playing football – one team in red shirts, the other in white and red stripes.

A woman in a woollen hat comes into the garden, beneath the limbs of the arboretum, followed by a coterie of lime green parakeets. Perhaps she is going to feed them or perhaps they are about to drill down and attack her hat?

A pinky golden apocalyptic light. The grass now empty of schoolboy footballers; Alec Guinness as George Smiley in his galoshes on the touchline of the playing fields in *Tinker Tailor Soldier Spy*. The sunset glow catching in the last yellow leaves of the ginkgo and maple and against the scabby-barked trunks of the already denuded plane trees. A squirrel bounding through the shrubbery beds.

As night settles – this will be tonight's dream. The lost garden found and then lost, and now having been refound, voluntarily given up to be lost again.

Belgrade Road café, Dalston. 5/12/18.

Yesterday, on the third day of our mini-vacation, Joseph and I took
the bus to Tooting. I showed him the pair of indoor markets either
side of Aldi's – and then walking along the High Street, both of us
needing a pee, I suggested we snuck into a café to sort out potential
dates for going to Australia in April. Buoyed up, our bladders
comfortable – the potential dates for flights scheduled in Joseph's
notebook – we enjoyed the kind patient way the East European
woman running the café allowed an elderly Englishman to tell her
all about why the Norwegians presented their best Christmas tree
each year to be put in Trafalgar Square – drawing a map on the table
with his finger: "This is the Strand. Here's Trafalgar Square."

The day before, we took the 'Wandle Trail', a path that wends
alongside the River Wandle from Earlsfield. Walking upstream
through the grimy industrial landscape to Collier's Wood – and then
surprised by beautiful parkland – boardwalks across bulrushed
marshes. Stopping for tea and a slab of plastic-encased Genoa
cake at the sports centre in Carshalton – the rain coming down
in a satisfyingly intense burst as we watched from the dry – the
swimming pool the other side of the glass next to our elbow.
Eventually (ten miles?) making it into Croydon – the chaos of Delta
Point, West Croydon station – *Blade Runner* city crushed into a
blender – and then the end of the route – Joseph insistent that we
slap the palms of our hands against the side of East Croydon station.

Churchyard, St Mary's, Battersea. 6/12/18.

A list of sights collects itself inside my head as I cycle along the Thames Path from Wandsworth Bridge in towards town. I stop to write them down before I drop any.

One. The older man dressed in black shirt and trousers – in one hand a just-begun cigarette, in the other an ice cream tub full of the crusted edges of bread that he flings up over the railings – each crescent neatly caught in the beak of one of the seagulls hovering there. A wry grin on the man's grizzled face; a satisfying daily ritual on his break from the kitchens of the riverfront restaurant.

Two. A small girl – three or four years old – unstoppably laughing at the immediate delight of living – as she stands on the strap at the back of the buggy in which her little brother is stacked below her; her laughter quite separate from her brother's more solemn state of mind or her father's – layered with preoccupations – pushing one-handed the handle of the buggy along the cobbled pavement outside the heliport.

Three. The orange wind cone in the heliport flying sturdily horizontal with a strong breeze off the river from the West.

Four. A real Christmas tree parked on the prow of a Thames barge anchored under a bridge – a wire of coloured light bulbs – red, yellow, blue and green – exactly like those in the permanent fir tree that used to be decked at the end of the driveway in Ipswich – lights that were kept the rest of the year coiled up in an old blue grey suitcase in the musty-apple-and-putty-smelling coach-house.

Five. A panel of glass being winched up by the crane on top of the forty storey diamond-shaped new building on the far bank of the Thames – opposite where I'm sat – here in the churchyard of St Mary's, Battersea.

In the twenty-five minutes that I've been here the dusk has fallen and the sodium orange streetlamps have popped on along both sides of the river – the even orangier-hued reflections elongating

35

out from the bank across the rumpled water to just above where the toes of my boots rest on the top of the small brick wall here in front of this churchyard bench – and the lamps on this side spill across the slick low tide mudflats. The apex of every construction crane lit with a red lamp – the one still working on the roof of the forty storey glass tower with a second red lamp flashing.

Perhaps next, after leaving Earlsfield, I'll live on a houseboat or a barge? Be the cheeky cabin boy – or, more age appropriately, the old sea salt with his smoking pipe on *L'Atalante*, the barge of Jean Vigo.

Keep moving. Keep rolling. Not yet time to set down permanent roots and begin to decay.

Passing a small tent planted on Clapham Common opposite the all-night burger stall by the big pond, the first few weeks of cycling home to Earlsfield from work, I joked to Joseph that my next move would be to just such a tent pitched on the Common – but now – beneath the corrugated roof of the park lock-up shelter near the entrance to the 'Winterville' entertainment fair – there are – last night I looked to make a tally of the number – nine or ten rough sleepers lain there in a row of sardines beneath duvets – a roof and two walls but otherwise open to the rain and the cold. I think of the Glaswegian man in his forties interviewed in The Guardian last week who came to London to beat his heroin addiction but still – nine months later – sleeps out on the streets – and who got a late night kicking from a group of drunken men which has left him partially blind in one eye. I think of them – the shadowy figures under the duvets. And of the one older black man who sits there – usually just him on his own – propped up against the back wall drinking from a can of stout when I cycle to work in the afternoon – and how delighted I was when after many attempts at trying to catch his gaze with a 'Good afternoon' or a nod of the head as I pedaled by – he for the first time clinked eyes with mine and then slowly tipped his chin a fraction forward and then a slow fraction back.

Outside the café in St. James's Park. 7/12/18.

'The role of the dreamer is to accept his dreams.'
Jean Cocteau

The images in the scrapbook – the violence of the side by side –
photos – music – voiceover – frames of celluloid repeated. The
reel snares and burns a hole. A symphony of coincidences. What is
politics? The schoolboy terrorists with their faces covered, cocking
their AK47s as they enter the assembly hall. Jean-Luc Godard's
latest film essay *Le Livre Des Images* plays in the small cinema at
the ICA – his croaky nicotine-gravelled voice explaining that even
if he knows it's almost impossible for our hopes to come true that
he must however go on hoping and believing in the possibilities
of a utopia. Another voice – the only female voice that appears
on the soundtrack – says that never do we tell the truths of what
man is doing to the world with enough sadness – and only when
we do begin to tell the truth with the deep vast amount of sadness
necessary will there be any possibility to begin to change it for the
better. James Stewart swims out to rescue the drowning Grace Kelly.
Black and white footage of a Nazi soldier dispatching – a bullet to
the head – each of a row of prisoners on the side of a boat – pushed
into the sea. Followed by phone footage of an Al Qaeda foot soldier
doing exactly the same – different gun, different boat, different
water – seventy years later.

The love we have is going nowhere.

Arthur Rimbaud, gun-runner and ex-poet rests his gangrened leg
and snuggles into the patchouli, sandalwood and hot salty-smelling,
semen-smeared chest of his Arabian lover. The investigative
journalist Jamal Khashoggi enters the Saudi embassy in Turkey
wired with a secret microphone. Through their headphones the
Turkish operatives hear the sounds of Khashoggi being murdered,
decapitated and sliced into small pieces that are then (CCTV
authenticated) spirited in a suitcase from the embassy onto a
waiting Saudi plane. The drugged political prisoners who were
dropped from army planes at night into the River Plate during
the dictatorship in Argentina – bodies found on the shores

37

of neighbouring Uruguay. 'How hard it is to sing when I must sing of horror' (Victor Jara, 'Stadio de Chile'). Consequences. Reverberations. Stop. Repeat. Losing track. A diamond-encrusted Emirates aeroplane. And then nothing. Sacks of refuse. I refuse. I refuge. The winter grip. The lights of Whitehall – Brexit debate – shimmering in the lake.

Old English Garden, Battersea Park. 8/12/18.

Stories that my eldest brother and his wife bring out at the dinner table when Joseph and I visit them in West Dulwich – about Dad and his various mishaps with DIY. Giving the flat roof at the back of the house in Rosendale Road a coat of bitumen, he took a step backwards, bringing down both the stepladder and the pot of bitumen that tipped itself over his head – so he came back inside covered in the gooey blackness – and we – Mum, the two of them, my sister and I burst into roars of laughter at the sight – much to Dad's chagrin.

Or when my sister-in-law went to pull the flush of the lavatory and the lid of the cistern dislodged and fell almost on top of her head and cracked the toilet bowl. Or when my other sister-in-law went to switch on a plug and the socket sparked and the electric shock threw her across the room and Dad said: 'Oh! I thought there was something a bit odd with that socket.' "And this," my brother laughed to Joseph, "was the man who used to be called in as an expert witness by the Institute of Electrical Engineers."

Saturday morning. On my way to work. The early blue sky shuttered out – in the walled garden in Battersea Park – trying to figure out how to make things more secure with Joseph. My head; his head; in which lies the doubts? Joseph in his messages last night – when I had picked up on the subliminal hint that he'd be going to blow off some steam after his shift – confirmed that yes, "I needed to get out of my head." And I had sent unanswered messages – booty call emails to the man on the fourteenth floor of the tower block in Southfields and to Sir in Crystal Palace.

Understanding myself – my sometimes need for pain to get to pleasure – those kinks – for all to see – sharing the fragility and robustness of the human condition – the balancing act of being true to your own needs and desires – whilst not hurting or transgressing those of the folk around you.

39

Harleyford Road Gardens, Vauxhall. 12/12/18.

The goldfish in the pond down in the grounds of this country
hotel – as big as those sharks in *Thunderball* – great big haunches
of orange and white, their fins flailing as they sparkle up from the
depths towards the surface. I look down from the mansard window
– leaning out – the slates biting cold to my grip.

"I'm not going to worry about Christmas this year," I tell myself,
"this Christmas-that-won't-be-Christmas with Joseph. We'll bypass
my annual seasonal bout of depression arm in arm." I suggest the
walk along the route that I cycled last night after my shift at Central
St Martins. Euston Road (a row of rough sleepers' tents along the
pavement under the overhang of an empty office block), Baker
Street, Oxford Street, Hyde Park – thousands of revellers decanted
from the 'Winter Wonderland' – a city of helter-skelter rides and
chairoplane carousels – LED bulbs above the iron perimeter fence –
Sloane Street, King's Road, Albert Bridge (is that its name – the pink
and white fairy light lit one?) – the path that meanders alongside
the river down to Wandsworth Bridge. An alternative to Christmas
with my Jewish boyfriend. Brussels sprouts, roast potatoes and a nut
roast.

I look down into the garden – the ornamental pond so full of goldfish
and carp – like in the Japanese garden near the Biblioteca Nacional
in Buenos Aires – but these are seeming to grow more and more
gigantic under my gaze – security lamps flooding the garden of the
hotel and illuminating the glittering whales bumping and nuzzling
into each other. And then – in this dream – aware that I have got
fixated on the menace of the goldfish – I step into my hotel bedroom
– a chambre de bonne under the sloping roof – and run a sinkful
of water to wash my face – the water cold turning to tepid, turning
back to cold. But the water doesn't run down the plughole and the
porcelain sink is full of undrained water – and three goldfish heads
peek up through the plughole. I look away – shuddering – and then
when I look back the three fish heads – their eyes and mouths open
– have no bodies attached to them and I realise that the rest of their
bodies have been eaten by the giant fish down in the pond – and

they just float there gasping for breath or food in the sinkful of water, which is when I wake up.

Goldfish have always freaked me out ever since we had a pond of them in the garden in Rosendale Road – inherited from the previous owner – and once when we came back from a two week summer holiday we found all thirty of them lying floating dead on the surface and Dad and I had to hook them all out with a spade and throw them in the bin (or possibly – my memory gives me alternatives – bury them at the end of the garden under the slowly dying peach tree).

Russell Square. 14/12/18.

Coming to write here on Tuesday evening, I told Joseph in the
City Lit canteen – when he creased his face as if I'd be mad to
try and sit here and write in the dark and the cold – that there's
something about the energies (leylines; the historical X of tracks; the
unexecuted plans for magical exhibitions by curators rushing to and
from the British Museum) that I find when I sit to write in Russell
Square, and that even the icy winter bite in the air is the opposite
of a hindrance – but rather galvanizes my brain to get my thoughts
marshalled into words and flung down – the nib of the biro across
the page – before the cold gets a grip on my toes and fingers, creeps
in under the waist of my jacket and frosts up my back. The man over
on the only other occupied bench in this ring – a reddish tinged
beard (colour night-time approximating) – scrolls his phone whilst
smoking from an electronic cigarette that has a wire curling from
the end of it into his canvas bag on his hip – so that he looks like the
caterpillar in *Alice In Wonderland* smoking on his hubble-bubble.
Another man, stacking the aluminium tables outside the park café,
sings with a loud out-of-key pummelling that can only mean he's
singing along to a Spotify shuffle pack of his favourite rock songs.

"'Carolling' is 'singing.'" Emily, my housemate, shows me the sign
language sign this morning – her forefinger wiggling a cord of
spirals upwards and away from the side of her mouth. She asks me
if I'll come carol singing with her fellow college students in Hoxton
tomorrow – and it's only when I've said 'Yes' that I remember that I
hate everything to do with Christmas. How can it spin around more
quickly each year until soon it feels I'll be putting my head down on
the pillow and waking up to one continual Christmas season that has
Donald Trump as Father Christmas and Theresa May as the Virgin
Mary, ad infinitum?

A couple walking by – pushing a small bobble-hat-wearing boy in
a pushchair – only the boy talking – a running commentary and
questions to his parents – the two of them only communicating with
each other through their four-year-old son.

Need to move – walk – chase the blood around my body – an ancient radiator thawing the chill of the early morning classroom.

Russell Square. One of the chefs wrenching open the gates in the railings at street level around the Russell Hotel – and hurrying down the iron staircase to the basement kitchens – allowing himself the luxury to pretend it's much colder than it really is – crunchy foot-deep newly fallen snow through which he has had to toboggan into work; Hercule Poirot, Paul Robeson and Vita Sackville West on the reservation list for the dining room tonight.

Harleyford Road Gardens, Vauxhall. 18/12/18.

Somewhere in childhood, the cut through Elton Park. The red and orange Ice Pops that my sister and I were only allowed to eat as a summer treat if we took them outside into the garden – the shard of ice in its envelope of clear plastic – the top sliced off with a pair of scissors – up into our mouths to suck on.

Tell your childhood with the muffled drumbeat of imminent peril of which at the time you were never aware. The anecdotal tales that could have ended grimly. "Do you remember that time you threw that pair of scissors at me?" my sister recalls.

When I met up with Alvaro a couple of years ago – three days in Madrid – he told me that walking through the Roma district of central Mexico City when he was a student he had seen an old woman struggling with several bags of grocery shopping – and so he had run up to her and asked if she would like some help. "She was old – in her late eighties," and he had carried her bags of shopping to the front door of her apartment. "And it was only the next day when I was at university that a professor called me over – "Alvaro," he said, "do you know who that woman was whose bags you were carrying in Roma yesterday? That was Leonora Carrington." The English artist, writer and longtime Mexican citizen who died in 2011.

Coming up the stairs from the Renoir screen of the Curzon Bloomsbury – Joseph in his oatmeal woollen trousers and his khaki winter coat – my hand warm and toasty between his two colder hands (funny – usually it's me that has colder hands than any lover's) – having seen Alfonso Cuarón's gorgeous semi-autobiographical movie about his family living in Roma in 1970 – I want to live inside the movie that seems to be happening to Joseph and I as we walk through the Brunswick Centre, along Marchmont Street – chatting in front of the illuminated window of books in 'Gay's The Word' – but also want to talk about how that movie reminded me of my own stay in Mexico City – the thirties courtyard in Tacubaya; the maid, Reina; sitting on the roof; the tortillas and tacos from street traders – and also of the apartments in the barrio of Caballito where I lived with Luke in Buenos Aires.

And then of how – as the movie portrays – in childhood the house you grow up in is a huge mighty kingdom in your imagination; and the garage where the car is parked, where the dog leaves its mounds of shit that the maid has to shovel up, wash and scour away with buckets of hot water. And only in young childhood do you saturate yourself in all the details and atmospheres of the different rooms of your home – only when you are young do you have the sufficient time and wonder to give the rooms – hallways, toilets and bathroom all equally significant – your full attention.

My bedroom. Earlsfield Road. 20/12/18.

Joseph has booked our plane tickets – travelling on Malaysia Airlines via Kuala Lumpur to Melbourne – flying mid-April and returning a month later. Joseph told me his mother mentioned that he would be bringing his 'friend' with him to her 94 year old mother. "My grandmother," Joseph laughed, "responded with a Yiddish saying which roughly translates as 'Every pot has its lid.'"

Sat in the café of the South London Gallery on Peckham Road – the long room out the back – glass sliding dormer windows that give out onto the garden – writing in my notebook as I waited for a bowl of carrot and ginger soup – feeling a bit achey and aguey with a newly but definitely arrived cold settling inside my body – I was about to tumble – free associate – into my notebook – the long wooden table cluttered with smudged glasses and cutlery and crumbed plates – when I heard footfall that I instantly recognized as being that of Joseph (he's a little heavy on his feet, heralding his approach and precluding him from ever being a cat burglar or ninja assassin) and he came along the passageway between the bookshop and the gallery and appeared – his coxcomb of dark hair newly waxed. "Oh, it's you!" – then, seeing the pen in my hand, "but don't let me disturb you." And I said: "No no, stay. I've just ordered myself some soup. If it tastes good we can order a bowl for you." The bowl of carrot and ginger soup arrived with a slice of sourdough toast drizzled with olive oil. I took a spoonful: "You've got to have some of this." I went and ordered a second bowl of soup for him.

I unpacked my cold and my weariness for Joseph. "How did you get a cold? We were doing so well!" "Yes," I said, "but I must have got a chill at work on Saturday. And I've been getting apprehensive about having nowhere to move to in less than two weeks."

Some brief passing moments of irritation with Joseph. Like when in the café on Marchmont Street he stood up and the hem of his jacket caught on the glass of brown sugar on the table next door – pulling it over and tipping a large amount of sugar onto the table and the floor – and instead of just sweeping up the sugar on the table, he did that, but then poured it back into the glass from his cupped hand –

46

apologizing to the man behind the counter – who was now probably going to have to throw away the whole glassful of sugar.

I had to hurry Joseph through his bowl of orange-coloured soup – his small spoonfuls that would linger in mid air as he told me about an email he had written to the union representative at his second job – I tugging up the cuff of his jumper to read the gold hand on the face of his grandfather's wristwatch. "We have to be there by 2.30?" "No," I said, "the ceremony starts at 2.30."

Crossing Peckham Road I saw a tall woman in a hat, a long coat over a pleated ankle-length crimson dress. "I'm sure she must be going to it." She stopped at the gates of No.34, checked her phone and then walked towards the side entrance of the Georgian terrace.

Inside, the African security guard welcomed us and ushered us into the reception area which was already thronged. The receptionist knocked on the glass and asked us to move along to allow a Colombian couple to fill in a certificate on the shelf there.

Mel and Alice's wonderful room of friends from their twenty years together, some from before. I tried to work out how long I have known Mel – but could only make a far from definite stab at twelve years. We walked across the hallway into a grander room of golden light. Alice, dressed in a tuxedo and black bowtie, made an announcement of how the ceremony would proceed once the doors were opened and they led the way into the other room.

I introduced Joseph to a friend from my writing group who said: "How lovely to meet you – we've heard so much about you – or rather your fictional alter ego. Although I must say – you are younger than I imagined you being."

I got a few degrees warmer; a feeling like trying to walk calmly across a room in front of a whole lot of important strangers only for one's shoes to snag on a ruck in the carpet. "No no," I said, "it's not that I've written lots about you." "That's fine," Joseph placed the flat of his hand on my sternum, "I know that's how you write. And that's why I think it better not to even want to read what you've written. That freedom's yours my sweets."

47

The double doors opened. Joseph and I took a seat with a side view of Mel and Alice stood in front of the registrar's table. The registrar, a Polish woman, made everyone laugh. "Without further ado, let's get on with Mel and Alice's citizenship – I mean," she giggled, "civil partnership."

The registrar had allowed Mel and Alice to slip in their own vows after the official ones – and to have time to read a poem that R V Bailey had written especially for them.

I have never seen both Mel and Alice so completely relaxed; not even a ripple of submerged tension – their wide eyes looking around the room at their thirty friends smiling back at them.

Joseph surreptitiously snapped some shots on his phone – our thighs rubbing snug together in the two chairs nearest the window out into the garden.

A recording of Barbara's brittle voice singing 'Je ne sais pas dire' as Mel, Alice, the Polish registrar, Mel's aunt and a friend from her teenage years curled forwards over the papers on the table to sign and witness their partnership. I remember what Neil Bartlett said about how his own civil partnership had made him feel surprisingly strong. When a man behind the wheel of a white van snarled 'You faggot!' as he had to slow to allow him across the road, Neil realised this less-than-24-hours-old new strength allowed him to shrug off this stranger's homophobic rage – his problem, not mine.

And outside in the garden of this Georgian house turned registry office – under a bower – photos were taken – one of all of us (the guest taking the photos swapping a couple of times), another of Mel and Alice and all their writing friends, and finally of Mel and Alice, arms around each other, unmistakably bound by several formats of love.

The Polish registrar welled up as she thanked Mel and Alice. "I don't want to cry on your wedding day." The security guard wished us farewell as we walked out along Peckham Road – a couple of blocks towards Camberwell Green – where we piled into the Lumberjack, a social enterprise café, for hot drinks.

Friends introduced themselves. A neighbour from Elephant and Castle; work colleagues from Mel's library; a speech therapist who had been there twenty years ago on the occasion that Mel and Alice had first met – who explained to Joseph and me as we stood waiting in the queue at the counter how she had intended to take a Santander bike to the registry office – but she had left it too late – and instead had taken a couple of buses – and asking the bus driver how to get there had had "one of those lovely London moments," when several passengers got involved to give her advice (some of it helpful but incorrect) until she was sure – yes – she was on the right bus – and this is where she wanted to get off.

And Joseph with his tall quiff of hair, Joseph who is so (seemingly) effortless in his abilities to open and keep conversations going – alighting on just the right detail. Me – clunky with the obvious one: "So..." pause, probably frowning, "what's your connection with Mel and Alice?"

Joseph is phenomenal. Who is it he says it to? It doesn't really matter – but just his observation: "We don't really do high drama together do we, sweets?" A squeeze of my hand. That lovely certainty.

Mel said – an addendum to Alice's impromptu thankyou speech in the basement of the Lumberjack – that she realised that in these difficult times we are living through, it's not just her but all of us who are struggling.

Old English Garden, Battersea Park. 27/12/18.

A wealthy family – three generations bundled up in woolly hats and scarves. The middle generation raise the volume of their already loud voices as they read out the names of the plants in the flowerbeds – just a few feet away from the homeless guy who sits on the same bench every day – the hood of his jacket up, his head slumped forwards so that none of his face shows – as if the loudness of their voices will shift the man or at least counteract the unease he makes them feel – as if they couldn't simply ask themselves 'What if this man were me?' and quietly pass him by, let him sleep in the wintery sunlight and have their loud family bonding session in another more open part of the park.

The bricks lain blotched with silver and green lichen – the gaps tufted with grass and sproutings of moss. Angela Carter's trick for continuing the momentum of a story – writing every day ten whole pages and stopping at the bottom of the tenth – coming back to what she had written the next day – reading over the first eight pages – putting a line through pages nine and ten – and continuing with renewed vigour from the final word in the bottom right hand corner of the previous day's eighth page. Angela Carter who came to talk to us – Olga Kenyon's Contemporary Literature class at Morley College in – what year would it have been – 1987? Those days of my true 'further education.' The clack of damp wood against damp wood as the wicket gate springs shut behind the departing family. A strutting magpie tossing aside a fallen leaf with contempt. And you who have nothing will need to look outside – and have a vaster world to contemplate than those with the plenty that keeps them trapped indoors - too scared to venture far into the world unaccompanied and alone. The sprig of holly tied to the struts of that bench. The fake faux sun. The homeless man – his hood now down – unpeeling an orange or his fingers venturing into a folder of rolling tobacco. His chesty cough. How many winters can that survive? The smell of citrus on his fingerless-gloved fingertips – a flame from his fingers – the roofless hall of this man's head.

(Un)common Space, Tate Britain. 29/12/18.

As the day comes closer – the 2nd or 3rd of January – I'm not exactly sure which – when I have to move out of the house in Earlsfield – I tell myself not to get anxious; to hold my nerve; not to compromise; that the right place will turn up – and in the meanwhile I can use this time in limbo – the state of being 'homeless' – to my advantage – to investigate other possibilities of existence in London – remembering how just last year Stéphane was floating about when his own flat was uninhabitable with no toilet or running water – and he stayed for several weeks in the hostel in Borough and occasionally slept in the entrance of the 24 hour Tesco on Morning Lane in Hackney; or a man I know who, addicted to playing the financial markets, hasn't a penny spare to pay for the hostel where he used to live and now spends every night hopping from the full length ride of one night bus onto another route, snoozing slumped in a seat, his head resting against the window – until he can go back to the public library, plug in his laptop and resume his ill-fated gamblings.

What I do know for certain is that I have to find my own solution. I have my pride – I don't want to feel beholden to friends to come up with an answer. And with friends there is often room for misunderstanding. A friend last Sunday said to me there's space in her studio for me to store my boxes – but when I checked in with her again last night she backtracked: "Oh – how much stuff is there? I haven't got room for a lot."

I overheard one of the fire officers in the canteen at the theatre yesterday evening saying she had worked three shifts volunteering for Crisis over the last week – and how they had been simply overwhelmed by the homeless people who turned up this year in far greater numbers than ever before.

And of course my situation is nothing like as bad as those guys sleeping rough on Clapham Common or in tents along Tottenham Court Road and Euston Road. I could – if I felt panicked or motivated enough – apply to the few flat and house shares on 'Spare Room' that don't preclude a 52 year old on the basis of age – £700, £800, £900 a month. I know how to live frugally – but not that frugally – meaning that more than half my wages goes directly on paying my rent.

Joseph seems more freaked about the whole thing than I am: "You have to find a place to live before you can do anything else." As if somehow he's holding himself back from getting too attached to someone who doesn't have the basic ability to take care of himself. And sure – we look to our elder friends to see how they cope – to learn from them, to pick up a few tricks and tips for our own future.

Look – watch me – I'll show you how it's done.

The self-belief – to hold your nerve and seek and wait – to feel that 'home' is a state of being that we each take with us, that comes into being through thought and sensory experience.

When I am cycling around London, my bike is my home. When I'm sat on park benches or in cafes or in galleries writing, my notebook is my home. When I am with Joseph and with my friends, the people I love are my home.

So – watch me – how I do it – a high wire act of derring-do with just the minimum of baggage: clothes, a spare set, toothbrush, this notebook, a couple of Biros, bike lights and locks, waterproofs. I'll make myself another chapter of my existence – old desire paths; accidents of the new; showering in the Turkish baths in Queensway; the heated lido on London Fields; Oasis at Holborn; sleep at Stéphane's; with Joseph; at Boris's; Ari's; an occasional night in a hostel – let's see – push against fear – which doors will open – which remain firmly closed? How much of what we think we really need is actually – live without it – not necessary at all?

Poetry Library, Royal Festival Hall. 17/1/19.

As Alex from the bookshop slices open his steak at one of the tables in the green room of the theatre he asks: "Was this his first time in Paris?"

I mishear. "Was this my first time?"

"No – not yours, for goodness' sake – Joseph's."

"Er – no – he's been there once before."

"And so what did you do?"

"We stayed in an apartment on the Rue de Charonne that belongs to a friend of his mum's. We went to see this play at the Théâtre de l'Odéon – *Les Idoles* by Christophe Honoré. And we did a lot of walking. And looking for vegan restaurants. Joseph's vegan."

"There's lots of vegan places in Paris aren't there?"

"Well – maybe. But not anywhere you can get a really nice pastry or croissant."

"You're not one of these couples who have to do everything together are you? I hate that."

"Oh no – I had plenty of croissants."

"Good. I must say it sounds very romantic – the two of you walking around Paris together."

"Romantic? Was it? Not really. Perhaps." (And yet it was).

The sky beneath the edge of the blind above the cubbyhole of this work station in the Poetry Library – a flock of seagulls rising and falling on the thermals.

And yet if it wasn't romantic (it was) what was it?

"On the final day – yesterday – my goodness – was it only yesterday...?" I continued the conversation with Alex in my head, "you see we came back this morning on the early train from Paris. Well, yesterday we kind of lost our mojo a bit and spent a couple of hours vacuuming, scrubbing the bathtub and just generally sprucing the flat up a bit – oh, it's on the seventh floor of this ten storey block – from the 1960s I guess – and you come out of the lift (Joseph took a photo of the make of the lift and sent it to his sister with the tag 'Schindler's Lift' – "Holocaust humour" he told me) and everything in the corridor is a different shade of beige and there are two slatted wooden chalet doors along the corridor – and when we first arrived the apartment smelt so musty inside – and there was mould growing in splodges over the toilet seat – it had been so long since the last person visited – it took the first day to open the shutters, unseal the dormer windows and blow some fresh air through the place.

And yesterday was our third day and we ran out of ideas and energy – and I was grumpy – and Joseph had suggested going to Versailles – and I said "Fine – let's go – but I don't want to go around the palace – I've been before – I'll find some place to sit and write," (which in truth would have been perfect), but Joseph said "Oh no – I don't want to go around on my own. I want to do it with you." And eventually we ended up taking the Metro to the Bois de Boulogne (explaining the scene when I arrived here with Kaz in August 1986 – the British Rail train to Folkestone, the Sealink ferry to Dieppe and the SNCF train to Gare Saint-Lazare, arriving in the middle of the night at the campsite – the ground as hard and dry as iron – hammering the tent pegs in with a block of stone – Kaz in the middle of her period). And Joseph and I picnicked on a damp toppled elm tree – on aubergine and tahini-spreaded baguette and some earthy tasting tomatoes.

A few hours later – walking along the Rue Saint Maur – a crowd of forty fetishistically shiny pompiers stood outside a bar – and – just before them – a crowd of black teenage boys. "We'll find out later what happens," said Joseph. In the Vietnamese restaurant where we ate, four 'Uber Eats' motorcyclists turned up one after another – all within ten minutes of each other – to collect the same order that the first motorcyclist had taken – the fourth one telling the Vietnamese waiters that the first courier was a fraudster, "un voleur!"

And passing back the same way an hour and a half later, all sign of the dazzlingly polished pompiers had vanished into thin air – but the twenty or so teenage boys were still there. Joseph took a detour a few steps over to the side and around the trunk of a tree – coming back to my side as we passed the last young man who, having registered Joseph's nervous diversion, turned to call to us "Peace and love", holding up two fingers. Embarrassed, I held two fingers up and waved them over my shoulder. "Are you OK?" I squeezed Joseph's hand. "Yes, I'm fine." As a young black man, how not to get angry to be read that way? As a queer man bullied and intimidated growing up how not to transmit your fears?

This morning – up long before dawn to return the apartment keys to the estate agents – I noticed one bank with its windows all replaced with wooden boards – a fly poster glued to it announcing BON RESOLUTION 2019. An occasional fraught outburst; an overly aggressive beggar on the Metro – or the security guard shoving a man on the concourse at Gare du Nord who was panhandling the queue at 'Paul' coffee stall; another homeless man remonstrating with the guard. The keys through a letterbox; the number pad in polished brass.

Joseph getting me to ask in French at the Jewish bakery if any of the pastries were 'Parve.' "Parve?" I questioned him. "Just ask." And the lips of the tall woman behind the counter instantly opened to show a radiant smile – as she gestured along the length of the glass counter: "All of these are Parve."

What else happens? Joseph and I snuggled up – our un-shoed feet sandwiched together – in the cinema up a flight of stairs on the Place de la Bastille. Walking for miles – on Tuesday – the Highline green walkway, around the grass-sloped walls of the Palais Omnisports at Bercy where I sang in a Beethoven spectacular in the Spring of 1988 – the conductor, Lorin Maazel, bouncing on the podium in a pair of white and gold trimmed sports sneakers made by one of the sponsors of the concert. Across a footbridge, past the twin towers of the Bibliotheque Nationale; through the Jardins des Plantes; into the Jardins de Luxembourg – those pale green iron chairs around the ornamental pond – explaining it to Joseph – imagine it on a summer's evening – coming here to read – the children nudging their toy yachts with canes across the surface. The Medici fountain at present drained of water.

Getting narky with Joseph; Joseph being brittle. And all of our permutations that are able to coexist.

Two single beds in the apartment that Joseph shoves together that he suggests we sleep across – and I say "No no – not that way – we'll sleep across the crack and our backs will hurt in the morning. Let's sleep side by side. And then you can come across to my island or I can come across to yours." No curtains at the window – so we can see across to the skyline of the Bastille and the spotlight strafing from the top of the Eiffel Tower, fizzing with silvery spangles.

The first place Joseph and I chose to visit – just ten minutes' walk from the flat – Père Lachaise. "Are you sure it's not too bleak a place to visit on a grey day?" I hesitated. But happily Joseph is not afraid of cemeteries. And looking for Edith Piaf's grave (one that with Joseph's app-happy phone took a tenth of the time it took Kaz and me to locate thirty two years ago) we happened upon a memorial to those who had died at Ravensbrück concentration camp. "Which is where my grandmother – " Joseph explained, "my father's mother – was liberated from." And went on to find Oscar Wilde's memorial, walled up in glass – the glass lipsticked with lip-prints; cigarettes, Metro tickets and carnations posted in through the gap. A lone red rose wilting on the black marble gravestone of the various Prousts buried with Marcel. "Oh," I said, pointing Joseph to his dates, "he was a year younger than I am now when he died. I really need to get a move on." Joseph narrowed his eyes at me. "I mean – to read all of *Á la recherche du temps perdu.*"

Joseph scolding me when I bite my fingertips – and last thing at night in bed, rubs the palms of my hands and my fingers with moisturising cream. Of such care is romance in Paris made. Oh – and him noticing a shop that sells shoelaces and coaxing me inside – a shoebox of different coloured laces on the counter – until I choose some glittery thin neon blue ones, so that we each take one of my hot moist-inside shoes to relace as we wait for the movie to start in the rundown Bastille cinema.

Fordham Park, Deptford. 25/1/19.

Cycling to Joseph's in the evening after work – coming off the
Quietway after the path wheels around behind the back of the Den
– the Millwall stadium and the railway lines – gantries of power
lamps hovering over the pitch glowing yellow to fool the grass
into believing it is warm daylight – to photosynthesise and lushly
grow to impress the away team and the fans when they arrive on
Saturday afternoon: 'Wish we had a pitch halfway as decent as this.'
The crevices between the hillside and the outer wall of the stadium
are used to home a fleet of coaches and a builders' skip disposal
depot – the commercial imperatives of a football club precariously
yo-yoing between the third and the giddy heights of the first division
and back again. Under the bridge and alongside the industrial park
– the smoke-and-steam-belching castle of the so-called recycling
but in fact mainly burning-rubbish-for-energy plant. Past a gated
yard of railway viaducts that seem to double at the weekends as rave
pop-up clubs and Pentecostal churches. Coming off the Quietway
– before it goes through the park and on towards Deptford High
Street – I cycle down the road that turns left and bear right, up the
lowered lip of the pavement opposite and under the trees – carob,
witch hazel, plane – of Deptford Green. A path that is lit up with grey
sci-fi streetlamps bent over horizontal at the fifteen foot mark – a
downward oblong of white light – each Triffid-shaped lamp with a
red jelly eye on the end – that only last night I figured might be in
case the Whitechapel Hospital helicopter needs to set itself down
on this wide expanse of grass – or for a fleet of Martian spaceships
to land, its personnel fanning out towards Lewisham and Peckham.
Joggers, dogwalkers, flâneurs and flâneuses coexist. The curlicuing
scent of a hashish-crumbled roll-up. A man on roller skates intently
choreographing himself a routine beside the basketball court – his
boombox on the concrete ping pong table. All this flood of good
vibes – a secret pocket of London's energy – on – past the floating
wooden posts of the adventure playground – across the road and
the underpass beneath New Cross train station – Walpole Road – a
flash of steam-punk in the purple and amber lights and cookie-
cutter ironwork of the tunnel – and on along the path – Somebody
McMillan's Park – trees and grass – the strideway between Deptford
Waste Market and the station that always has folk along it 24 hours

of the day. The cycle stands – mine nearly always the only bike left there beside the lavender bushes. That little extra buzz as – having clicked my locks around the wheels – I lift my knapsack onto my shoulders and walk to the protective interior of Joseph and Flo's kingdom – Deptford cracking open as an adoptive home. Joseph going to work for the early shift at eight this morning – tugging the end of the duvet to cover my feet and then smacking a kiss on my sleeping cheek – not my mouth (sour morning breath?) – before letting himself out of the front door.

Russell Square. 28/1/19.

Getting off the 188 before my intended stop – about to pee myself
– running up the steps at the back of the Festival Hall – and into
the main floor foyer – degree ceremony black gowns and mortar
boards – new Antisocial Behaviour notices stuck to the wall in the
Gents – before I catch a Thomas Heatherwick designed Routemaster
double decker bus to Russell Square (Thomas Heatherwick – a name
I always mix up with the openly gay British/Polish TV weatherman
Tomasz Schafernaker, who lost his job or at least was suspended
from the BBC weather bulletins after he stuck his middle finger
up at the news anchorman who made some snarky remark in the
handover to the weather room – Schafernaker's middle finger
tucked away just a fraction too late and caught on telly screens in
outraged living rooms up and down the country). And sure – I'm not
really a fan of his design – too much maroon plastic and the basic
mistake of no wind-down windows so that when the bus is full and
busy the air is hot and zinging with fetid germs – but I do enjoy the
curved sides of the roof and the Cinemascope front window on the
top deck. The day-off-cyclist's luxurious treat of six or seven stops
along the 68 route – enough time to sink into a chapter of the book
I'm reading (Sam Fisher's *The Chameleon*, the main character a book
who shapeshifts its title and contents, sponging up details from
its owners' lives). And getting off at Russell Square – the denuded
almost bald soil fenced off and seeded with grass that pops up in
neat segregated straight lines – just like the follicles of hair that
Mr P, my A level English teacher, had transplanted into his scalp in
1982. Mr P who was constantly blowing his nose and read out with
tongue-rolling relish all the most ribald lines of *The Canterbury
Tales*. I hid my smile when he explained that 'gat-toothed' (as
in, someone with a gap between their middle front top teeth in
Chaucer's London) signified someone who was believed to be
particularly lusty. Mr P who was seen by Nat and Finola dancing his
socks off in Heaven under the arches of Charing Cross one Saturday
night and who took a summer term off to go and teach at a school
in San Francisco. Would that he had been able to talk to us (to me)
about his life as a gay man in Thatcher's bleak land. His impressions
(what he got up to?) of pre- (but only just?) Aids San Francisco. I
don't remember him outing himself to us – his small A level set. It

was a time when gay teachers stayed in the closet. The year after we left another gay teacher at our school was arrested for 'antisocial behaviour' – cottaging at a public convenience in Tulse Hill – and was immediately sacked.

The crisp cold sinks its teeth into my bladder – and I stick to the circular macadam path – noticing the first blinks of mauve and yellow crocuses snatching at the sunlight as I exit the square – the cabbies' green hut offering soup and a roll for £3.50 – into the youthful courtyard in front of SOAS – and across to Birkbeck – through the revolving doors and down to the basement toilets – stragglers dribbling into an already-started lecture across the hall. The brisk ten minute walk to Birkbeck and back joggles up my blood and pushes it to visit my toes and fingertips – a tall young man's immense legs two steps ahead of me up the steps from the basement also doing their bit to pump my heart a little faster. The toasty smell of a photocopying machine. The brazen cigarettes smoked in the courtyard. I wonder whether to side track to Gordon Square, momentarily a shy poet invited to a 'sharing' at Virginia and Leonard Woolf's – or to say hello to the bronze lungi-wearing Mahatma Gandhi in Tavistock Square – but no – not a serious temptation – the same bench calls me back lacquered in the last twenty minutes of plunging sun.

A group of teenagers in sports kit – two of the boys in shorts – how is that even possible in this bitter cold? – string out along the southern edge of the square. An elderly man in a flat cap, long black coat and brown corduroys has to step around them – enunciates clearly the word "Bitch!" at the nearest girl, the only black person in the party. She turns: "Excuse me?" she challenges. The man stalks off pretending not to hear. The girl breathes deep and calls across the square – the icy air allowing her words to travel with ringing clarity and victorious purpose: "OLD MAN, YOU SHOULD BE ASHAMED OF YOURSELF."

South Bank, outside the National Theatre. 31/1/19.

And there outside outside outside – the lines where the ice has been
crunched by boots on Deptford Green and refrozen overnight. 'Is
it snowing?' Mel asks in an email from her mother's garden study
shed in Wellington, New Zealand. 'Not yet,' I write back, 'just crisp
and dry.' But too cold to linger there after the glow of the coffee from
'LP' on New Cross Road has done its brief warming tour of my body
– the counter loaded with a Pyrex glass dish of just-baked pumpkin,
broccoli and tomato frittata – a woman my age my age my age sitting
on a bar stool reminiscing about the Turkish shop next door but one
where she used to buy all her fruit and veg – chatting to the long-
grey-haired man sat with his crutch balancing against the lip of the
counter – the man Joseph reckons is the owner of the café. Joseph
who left in the dark to go to an early early shift – me guiltily sleeping
in – and then rising to pack a pound shop holdall into his huge
suitcase that I'll wheel along to the station and onto the Victoria
line to Seven Sisters and to my new home tomorrow at noon. Me
enraptured by the fair-haired young man behind the counter at 'LP'
busy spooning baked beans from one almost empty Tupperware box
into another almost full one – and then sliding the full box into an
empty slot in the glass-fronted fridge – who when I went on my own
a week or two ago regaled his every brief interaction with me with
a melt-your-socks-off smile – but who today only had eyes for the
baked beans.

And last night – again sniffing my woollen scarf when I got to
Joseph's – the curious smell of smoke – as if I had been through
a bonfire. Joseph leaning in to kiss me a few nights before had
questioned whether I'd had a sneaky cigarette on my way home –
and last night I twigged – the Bermondsey recycling plant that is
actually mostly a giant incinerator burning waste – and this odour
– Dad's beloved pyromaniacal bonfires in the garden in Ipswich
on Sunday afternoons – must come from that white smoke peeling
up against the clear black blue winter night sky. And here on the
South Bank five young Korean men in snappy day-glo coloured
clothes – one with a mop top of bleach blond hair – pose in various
combinations against the Thames railings – like K-Pop princes. And
I'm not sure anymore of anything anything anything. 'Why are young

men killing each other?' asks a poster slapped with paste to the glass of the bus stop in New Cross Road. The jogger's bullet of spit that he launches just as he comes parallel with me – sat on this 'Everyone Needs A Place To Think' bench.

Belgrade Road café. 26/3/19.

With Joseph's help (oh, how a person can arrive as if from nowhere and with just their presence transform the fabric – the whole being of your day to day life) I get my bedroom into some sort of shape – stack boxes of notebooks and papers into columns at the foot of my bed and tucked between the side of the wardrobe and the radiator so that there will be some space for when I transport more boxes of books, LPs, packets of photos and folders of juvenilia over from Ari and Karsten's on Monday.

"This folder is from 1985," I said, pulling out a fat faded salmon pink manila folder of snippets of writing that I had typed up on Mum's old Brother typewriter. "I was two then!" said Joseph cheekily – and took off his shoes, shuffled his bottom back onto the mattress, lowered his head onto the pillow, swung his legs up and pulled the duvet up over his shoulders: "I'm just going to rest my eyes for a few minutes," – lying there in bed snoozing; his long dark eyelashes entwined and the freckles over his nose and cheekbones; eyes firmly but relaxedly sealed; his regular breathing and his pretty loveliness such a joyful peaceful presence in my room as I shoved and lugged boxes around, stacking paperbacks like a fishmonger grabbing a handful of trout into the small bookcase – the tips of Joseph's toes on one foot peeking out from the bedclothes – mine a cold room even with the plug-in extra radiator shoving out heat – so that I gave his foot a squeeze before I wrapped the duvet cover over his feet and tucked them in. And of course I teased him when after an hour he woke up – about how very much he had helped me get my room sorted – and he reckoned that "I've just been lying here for ten minutes with my eyes closed. I wasn't actually asleep."

And on Monday morning, walking over to Ari and Karsten's, picking up a box of jam doughnuts (vegan) from Percy Ingle – Ari up in the roof passing my boxes down – I stood on the ladder, handing the boxes into the arms of Joseph and Karsten, the comb of a wasp's nest fallen in dusty chunks into several of the boxes.

ACKNOWLEDGMENTS

To Christina Petrie for her wise and acute editing; for her support and encouragement to hold my nerve and see this project through to publication.

To Simon for all his kind support and sparky loveliness.

To my writing gang; especially the guidance and belief of Christina Dunhill. To Mia Farlane and Alan McCormick for close readings of the text. And to Mark Blackburn and Emma Sawyer.

To Pipe Vrdoljak whose café has been such a calm haven these last five years.

To Nicholas Wand for magicking up design and layout.

To Arthur Stitt at Calverts and Alma and Pari at Fedrigoni.

To Madhia Hussain, Kristen Phillips and David Curry.

To everyone who got caught up in the ride intentionally or not. And apologies to anyone caught unawares.

And remembering everyone sleeping rough in London tonight. All proceeds from this pamphlet go to CRISIS.

To share comments and feedback; to get in touch with the author; to order copies or for large print or an audio version of the text please email: reuben_lane@protonmail.com